Instant Adobe Edge Inspect Starter

Step-by-step, hands-on recipes to debug, test, and preview web applications on multiple mobile devices with Adobe Edge Inspect

Joseph Khan

BIRMINGHAM - MUMBAI

Instant Adobe Edge Inspect Starter

First published: February 2013

Production Reference: 1150213

Published by Packt Publishing Ltd.
Livery Place
35 Livery Street
Birmingham B3 2PB, UK.

ISBN 978-1-84969-400-1

www.packtpub.com

Credits

Author

Joseph Khan

Reviewer

Christopher Tilford

Acquisition Editor

Wilson D'souza

Commissioning Editor

Meeta Rajani

Technical Editor

Charmaine Pereira

Project Coordinator

Priya Sharma

Esha Thakker

Proofreader

Maria Gould

Production Coordinator

Melwyn D'sa

Cover Work

Melwyn D'sa

Cover Image

Conidon Miranda

About the Author

Joseph Khan is a Senior Web Developer at GoldSpot Media where he specializes in mobile web apps, rich media apps, and other **RIAs (Rich Internet Applications)**. Before moving into mobile web development he was working with Adobe Flex, Action Script, and Flash technologies and developed data visualization and enterprise dashboard based applications for clients such as Cisco, The World Bank, AADI, and other global organizations. His liking towards mobile web development has been recent and he has been hooked ever since. He also likes Phonegap, SASS, Drupal, and Python.

He has a Bachelor's degree in Computer Science from N.I.T Silchar, India and has been working on the Web and related technologies for 6 years.

Besides his regular work he also likes to design cars and motorbikes, ride his Yamaha, and look for good food. Find out more about him and all his work at http://jbkflex.wordpress.com/.

I would like to dedicate this book to my parents, my wife without whom I would not have been here, and specially to my newly born baby boy 'Ayaan'.

About the Reviewer

Christopher Tilford has a degree in English Literature, and aside from writing and literature, Christopher has been a freelance graphic and web designer for over 6 years. He founded AzurePro Studios in 2006 as a way for him to bring life to his own creative ideas. Over the years he has met numerous creative individuals and has developed an extensive network of talented connections.

Christopher has a background in advertising and brings his creative flair and enthusiasm to the table. An avid creative enthusiast, he is the author of *Shattered Heaven: Sins of the Soul* and its subsequent three sequel novels. He took up screenwriting in 2007 when he began to venture into animation. Not just a writer, Christopher has made it his joy to become proficient in all things Adobe. From writing to graphic design and animation, Christopher has set no limits to what he would like to accomplish. You can find out more about him and his work at http://www.azureprostudios.com.

www.packtpub.com

Support files, eBooks, discount offers and more

You might want to visit www.PacktPub.com for support files and downloads related to your book.

Did you know that Packt offers eBook versions of every book published, with PDF and ePub files available? You can upgrade to the eBook version at www.PacktPub.com and as a print book customer, you are entitled to a discount on the eBook copy. Get in touch with us at service@packtpub.com for more details.

At www.PacktPub.com, you can also read a collection of free technical articles, sign up for a range of free newsletters and receive exclusive discounts and offers on Packt books and eBooks.

www.packtLib.packtpub.com

Do you need instant solutions to your IT questions? PacktLib is Packt's online digital book library. Here, you can access, read and search across Packt's entire library of books.

Why Subscribe?

+ Fully searchable across every book published by Packt
+ Copy and paste, print and bookmark content
+ On demand and accessible via web browser

Free Access for Packt account holders

If you have an account with Packt at www.PacktPub.com, you can use this to access PacktLib today and view nine entirely free books. Simply use your login credentials for immediate access.

Table of Contents

Instant Adobe Edge Inspect Starter

Welcome to *Instant Adobe Edge Inspect Starter*.

This book has been especially created to provide you with all the information you need to get up to speed with testing and debugging web pages and applications targeted for mobile browsers. This book is a practical, hands-on guide that provides you with a number of detailed steps that will help you to get started on testing and previewing all your mobile web projects on multiple mobile devices. This book will also show you how to use all the other available features of Edge Inspect and make the entire testing process on a mobile device very simple, effortless, and faster.

This document contains the following sections:

So, what is Adobe Edge Inspect? – Find out what Edge Inspect actually is, what you can do with it, and why it's so great.

Installation – Learn how to download and install Adobe Edge Inspect with minimum fuss and then set it up so that you can use it as soon as possible.

Quick start – pairing mobile devices with your computer – This section will show you how to perform one of the core tasks of remote debugging of a mobile web application with Adobe Edge Inspect, for example, pairing and connecting test mobile devices with a computer.

Top 7 features you'll want to know about – Here you will learn how to perform seven tasks with the most important features of Adobe Edge Inspect. By the end of this section, you will be able to perform remote previewing, debugging, and testing of mobile web pages on multiple mobile devices remotely from your computer to ensure that your mobile web page looks as intended across devices that you have targeted for your audience. You will also learn to perform some other commonly used features of Edge Inspect such as taking live screenshots of the application running in all the mobile devices and so on.

People and places you should get to know – This section provides you with many useful links to the official sites and forums of Adobe Edge Inspect, as well as a number of helpful articles, tutorials, blogs, Facebook, and Twitter pages.

So, what is Adobe Edge Inspect?

Adobe Edge Inspect (previously known as Adobe Shadow) is a preview and inspection tool that helps frontend web developers and designers to develop and test web projects targeting mobile web browsers. With Adobe Edge Inspect you can pair multiple mobile devices and browse in sync with your computer, remotely inspect and debug your mobile web projects, make changes to the HTML markup, CSS style rules, and JavaScript, and instantly see the changes in the targeted mobile devices. This ensures that your mobile web page looks as intended across the multiple mobile devices that you are targeting for your audience.

Reasons for using Adobe Edge Inspect

Normally when you develop a mobile web application, you first debug and test the changes in your computer browser. I used to do this but found these three major problems with the traditional way of debugging for mobile web applications:

+ **Resolution issues**: Your mobile device is much smaller than your computer. So while testing it in your computer browser you have to restrict it to a particular resolution/ size to replicate the targeted mobile device. But if you are testing for multiple mobile devices of different resolutions then it becomes difficult to change the size values every time you test it in your computer browser. To make things worse, sometimes even the changes made in your computer browser are not reflected accurately on the mobile device.

+ **Touch events**: Your mobile web application will normally use JavaScript touch events, for example, if you are creating some kind of animation app that relies on finger touch gestures. So if you are testing your application in a computer browser then you have to map those touch events to mouse events and then again map it back to touch events when viewing on a mobile device. This is cumbersome until you have an automatic way of detecting the touch capability of the device browser and then handle the events accordingly.

+ **Lack of a web inspector in mobile browsers**: There is no real web inspection tool such as a Firebug or a Chrome developer tool in a mobile web browser. All that you can do is run the mobile web application in a computer browser and use its web inspector to debug it. But that does not actually help in terms of viewing the changes directly on the mobile device and you do not know how it will look on the mobile device itself.

So, if you are a developer or a designer targeting mobile browsers and you have faced these issues before then you can thank Adobe Edge Inspect as it directly handles all of them.

What you can do with Adobe Edge Inspect

At the time of writing this book, Adobe Edge Inspect is targeted only for Webkit-based mobile browsers and Adobe has supported only Apple iOS and Google Android devices. So, as of now, you can test only on these two types of devices. This is one downside of Edge Inspect but nevertheless major and popular mobile platforms prefer the Webkit-based browsers, and mobile Webkit is the way to go for mobile browsers.

As an example, see the following image, which shows multiple mobile devices (an iPod Touch, an Android phone, and an iPad) being paired to my computer with Adobe Edge Inspect over a wireless network and how a page (I have chosen the Edge Inspect home page `http://html.adobe.com/edge/inspect/`) opened on my computer browser is in sync with all the connected mobile devices. This is what Edge Inspect does—it will instantly preview the web page in all your targeted mobile devices and you will immediately know how it looks. It also provides familiar inspection tools with which you can debug your application.

You can see that the layout and the design of the page changes automatically on the mobile devices (of course, your page has to implement that logic, for example, by using CSS3 media queries). I mentioned it here just to say that Edge Inspect can detect such responsive CSS designs and render the page accordingly in mobile devices.

Now, to remotely inspect and test the page, you can target any paired mobile device from the list, make changes to the HTML/CSS/JavaScript on your computer using familiar debugging tools, and see the changes being updated directly in your device in real time.

We will talk about this in detail in the *Quick start – pairing mobile devices with your computer* and *Top 7 features you'll want to know about* sections of this book.

Some features of Edge Inspect

Let's quickly check out what else we can do with Adobe Edge Inspect:

- ✦ **Screenshot**: Take a screenshot of the page opened on any or all of the connected devices from your computer.
- ✦ **Cache**: You can clear the cache on any or all of the devices from your computer itself.
- ✦ **SSL support**: Adobe Edge Inspect supports pages with certificates. Connected Edge Inspect devices will provide a dialog prompting you to accept an unsigned certificate.
- ✦ **Run full screen on mobile devices**: You can toggle full screen display on all paired mobile devices so that more of the real estate is available for testing.

There are several other features that we will talk about in detail in later chapters including the ones mentioned here.

Installation

In three easy steps, you can install Adobe Edge Inspect and get it set up on your system.

Step 1 – what do I need? (basic requirements)

Before you install Adobe Edge Inspect, you will need to check whether you have the basic minimum requirements, as listed in this step. These are the current specs at the time of writing this book.

Windows

+ Intel Pentium 4 or AMD Athlon 64 processor
+ Windows 7 or Windows 8 (Adobe Edge Inspect is currently not supported by Windows XP)
+ 512 MB of RAM
+ 200 MB of available hard disk space for installation of the Edge Inspect helper application
+ 1280 x 800 display with 16-bit video card
+ Broadband Wi-Fi Internet connection

Mac OS

+ Multicore Intel processor
+ Mac OS X v10.6 to 10.8
+ 512 MB of RAM
+ 200 MB of available hard disk space for the installation of the Edge Inspect helper application
+ 1280 x 800 display with 16-bit video card
+ Broadband Wi-Fi Internet connection

Google Chrome web browser

The Adobe Edge Inspect web inspector (the place where you will remotely test and debug) runs as a Google Chrome extension and you will need the Chrome web browser installed on your computer. The minimum version supported is Chrome 14 but for better results Chrome 21 or greater is recommended. So go ahead, download and install Google Chrome on your computer from this link: http://chrome.google.com/.

iOS

✦ Adobe Edge Inspect is compatible with iPhone (including iPhone5), iPod touch, and iPad

✦ iOS 4.3 or greater

✦ At least 2-3 MB of free storage on the iOS device

✦ Wi-Fi support

Android

✦ Android 2.1 or greater

✦ At least 2-3 MB of free storage on the Android device

✦ Wi-Fi support

Amazon's Kindle Fire support

The Edge Inspect application is available in the Amazon store for Android. You can download and install the app on Kindle Fire devices. You should have the following specifications:

✦ Android 2.1 or greater

✦ 740 KB of minimum free space

✦ Wi-Fi support

Step 2 – downloading and installing Adobe Edge Inspect

Adobe Edge Inspect is a part of Adobe Edge Tools and Services. You can get Edge Inspect by signing up for a free or a paid Creative Cloud membership subscription. With a free subscription you can download the free version of the Edge Inspect application and get started. The difference between the free version and the full version is that with the free version you can pair and connect only one mobile device with your computer whereas with the paid full version you can connect unlimited number of mobile devices with your computer simultaneously. We will soon be talking about pairing and connecting mobile devices in our next section, so till then this might sound a little confusing to you. To get the full version of Edge Inspect you can either buy a full Creative Cloud membership or upgrade to a paid subscription for Edge Inspect only.

Navigate to this link `https://creative.adobe.com/join/starter` to sign in to your Adobe Creative Cloud account or create a new one if you do not have it already. After logging into your Creative Cloud account you can download Edge Inspect by following the link as shown in this screenshot:

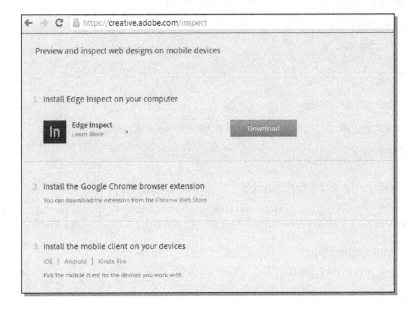

When you are downloading Edge Inspect it is the free version that you are downloading. You can upgrade to a full version by following the upgrade link below the download section. It is shown in the following screenshot:

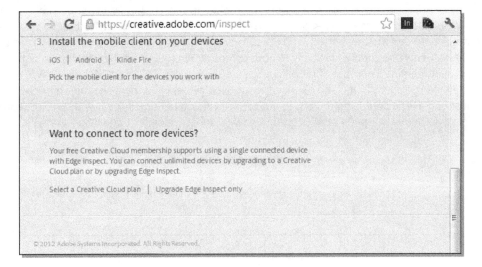

After that, it is very easy to set up Adobe Edge Inspect. There are four parts to setting up the environment. Let's look at each of them individually.

Edge Inspect application for your computer

The Edge Inspect application (I call it the helper application) runs on your computer. Download the installer from your Creative Cloud account for Mac or Windows based on the computer platform that you are using by clicking on the **Download** button shown on the previous page.

After downloading the installer file, locate it, and then run it. Follow the on-screen instructions in the setup wizard. The following image shows the installer setup on a Windows 7 machine:

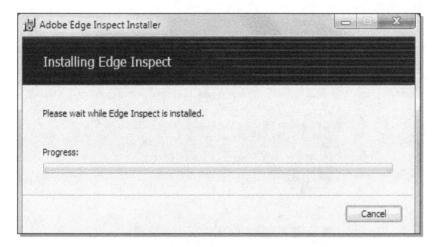

Similarly, if you are using a Mac machine, run the installer and follow the given instructions till you have the helper application installed on your computer. The overall steps for installation are pretty simple and you should be done within a few seconds.

After installing, you have to run this helper application in order to use Adobe Edge Inspect and start detecting devices. When you run it, it will live in the Taskbar Notification Area on Windows and the Menu Bar Extras on Mac OS X. We will talk more about this in our later sections.

Bonjour

Edge Inspect uses Bonjour for the auto-discovery and detection of target mobile devices. The Bonjour setup comes as a part of the Edge Inspect installation folder for Windows. So if you are using a Windows machine then go ahead and install it. You can find the Bonjour setup file as follows:

- ✦ Windows 32-bit machine:`\Program Files\Adobe\Adobe Edge Inspect\BonjourPSSetup.exe`
- ✦ Windows 64-bit machine: `\Program Files(x86)\Adobe\Adobe Edge Inspect\BonjourPSSetup.exe`

In Mac OS X, Bonjour is enabled by default so there is no need to install it separately.

Let's see what Bonjour is, before we move further. **Bonjour** is a network discovery technology developed by Apple Inc. that enables automatic discovery of devices and services on a local network. It is mostly used for finding printers and file-sharing servers, connecting them with a computer, and then using their services. You can learn more about Bonjour by visiting the official page at `http://www.apple.com/support/bonjour/`.

Edge Inspect client app for mobile device

The Edge Inspect mobile client will run on your mobile device. For each mobile device that you are going to test on, you will need to install the app on it.

✦ For an iOS device, navigate to the App Store and search for Adobe Edge Inspect, then download and install it. The following image shows the **Adobe Edge Inspect** app in the iOS app store:

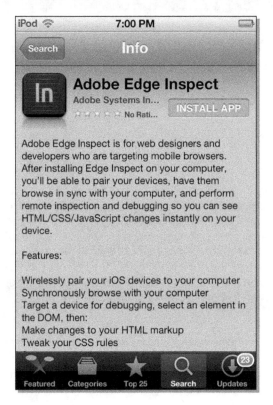

- For Android devices, navigate to Google Play (Android Marketplace is merged into Google Play) and search for Adobe Edge Inspect and then download and install it. The following image shows the Adobe Edge Inspect mobile app for Android:

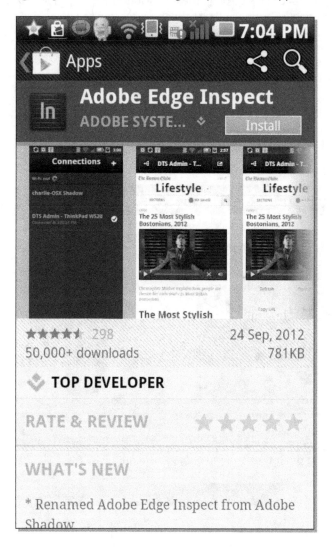

Both the iOS and Android apps are absolutely free, so go ahead and install them on your mobile devices. After you have installed the app it will appear as an icon with **In** written on it in your menu screen.

Google Chrome browser extension for Edge Inspect

You need to install the Chrome extension for Adobe Edge Inspect, as all interactions with the paired mobile devices take place through the extension. The Edge Inspect extension can be installed only with Google Chrome and no other browser. You can download the extension by following this link: `http://www.adobe.com/go/edgeinspect_chrome`. Click on the link to navigate to the Chrome web store and then click on the **ADD TO CHROME** button on the right to install the Edge Inspect extension.

After you install the Edge Inspect extension it appears as a dark grey icon with **In** written on it in the right-hand corner of Chrome's menu bar as shown in the following image:

Step 3 – installing a web server on your computer

As a developer you always want to test and debug your pages locally before moving them into production, so you need to download and install an HTTP web server on your computer. Edge Inspect cannot debug pages from the local filesystem via the file protocol (file:///). You will need to host your pages either in a local HTTP web server that runs on your computer or a hosted server that can serve your pages over the web. I am using the WAMP server on a Windows 7 computer and hosting all my mobile web projects inside the www folder. There are other options available for Windows; you can try something like XAMPP or the Apache HTTP server. If you are using Mac OS X, you can use the built-in Apache server to host your mobile web projects.

Download and install the WAMP server from http://www.wampserver.com/en/.

And that's it!

By this point, you should have a working installation of Adobe Edge Inspect and are free to play around and discover more about it.

Quick start – pairing mobile devices with your computer

Now that you have installed all the necessary components for Adobe Edge Inspect, let us see how to pair and connect mobile devices with a computer. You can wirelessly pair multiple iOS and Android devices to your computer and start the remote inspection of web pages running on the mobile devices.

First, make sure that your mobile device/devices and your computer are all in the same wireless network. This is important for the connectivity of the devices and performance.

The following step-by-step instructions will guide you.

Step 1 – start the Edge Inspect helper application on your computer

Launch the Edge Inspect helper application that you have installed on your computer. For Windows, go to the **Start** menu and search for Adobe Edge Inspect. You can see **Adobe Edge Inspect** in your search results. Click on it to run it. The following screenshot should help you:

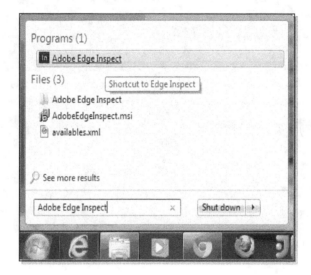

Similarly, for Mac users, search in the menu bar to look for Adobe Edge Inspect and then click on it to run it:

The Edge Inspect helper application (with **In** written on it) lives in the Taskbar Notification Area on a Windows machine as shown in the following screenshot:

On a Mac OS X machine the helper application resides in the top-right corner of the menu bar. The following screenshot shows Adobe Edge Inspect running on a Mac OS X computer:

After you have started the helper application on your computer you will notice that the Edge Inspect extension icon in your Google Chrome browser turns brown. This means that Adobe Edge Inspect is now activated on your computer.

Step 2 – start the Edge Inspect app on your mobile device

Look for the Edge Inspect client app with **In** written on it that you have installed on your mobile device and run it. It immediately autodiscovers the master computer via Bonjour and will list it under the available connections. The following screenshot shows the Edge Inspect app running on an iPhone and detecting my computer:

You can also manually add a computer by tapping on the "Add Connections" (**+**) button in the top-right corner, then entering the IP address, and then tapping on the **Join** button. The following screenshot shows it:

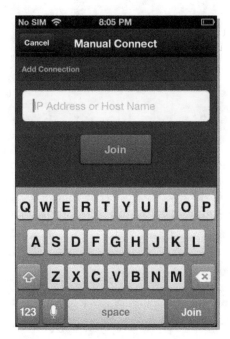

Step 3 – tap on the detected computer name to connect

Now, tap on the detected computer name (**joseph-PC**, in my case) on your mobile device and it will give you a passcode number. You will have to enter this number in the Edge Inspect browser extension in Chrome to authorize the connection. The following screenshot shows the passcode number on the iPhone:

Step 4 – enter the passcode number and authorize the connection

Click on the Edge Inspect extension icon in Google Chrome on your computer to open a pop-up dialog. You will see your mobile device listed there. You will also notice a textbox asking for the passcode number. Fill up the textbox with the passcode number that appears on your mobile device and then click on the **Authorize** button to pair. The following screenshot describes the step:

Step 5 – your mobile device is now paired

After you have authorized the connection, your mobile device is now paired with your computer. You can see your mobile device name on the list of paired devices.

After your mobile device is paired with your computer you can immediately see that whatever page is opened in Chrome on your computer, the same page is opened on your mobile device. There are some exceptions, though, such as a page that requires authentication or an SSL certificate acceptance, which we will talk about later in the *Top 7 features you'll want to know about* section. The Edge Inspect extension keeps track of the URL in your computer browser and sends it to the Edge Inspect app running on your mobile device. This URL is then opened in the Edge Inspect app.

Step 6 – pairing multiple devices

You can pair multiple iOS and Android devices to your liking with your computer. With the Edge Inspect helper application running in your computer follow step 2 through step 4 to connect and pair more mobile devices. The following screenshot shows an iPod Touch, an Android phone, an iPhone, and an Android tablet device paired to my computer:

So, in this section we have learnt how to pair mobile devices with the master computer. The next section describes in detail how to target a mobile device for remote inspection and debugging. There are several other features as well and I have that all in store for you in our next section.

Top 7 features you'll want to know about

As you start to use Adobe Edge Inspect, you will realize that there are a wide variety of things that you can do with it. This section will teach you all about the most commonly performed tasks and most commonly used features in Adobe Edge Inspect.

Remotely inspecting and debugging mobile web pages

With Adobe Edge Inspect you browse in Google Chrome on your computer and all the paired mobile devices stay in sync. This means that any page you open in Chrome either from your local HTTP web server (via localhost) or a production server, that same page is opened synchronously in all the paired mobile devices. After that you can target any mobile device for inspection and start remote debugging.

In this section, I will talk about the most important feature of Adobe Edge Inspect, that is, how we can remotely inspect and debug a mobile web page. First, let's create a simple demo application for our testing purpose. After that we will go step-by-step into debugging.

Creating a sample mobile web application page for our testing purpose

Remember that in the *Installation* section, we talked about installing a local HTTP web server on our computer for development and testing purpose. As a frontend developer developing for mobile devices, I always prefer to test things out in a local development environment before moving things into production, and since Adobe Edge Inspect can open pages from localhost we are going to run and debug our demo application from our local web server.

Our demo application will be a very simple structured HTML page targeted for mobile browsers. The main purpose behind building it is to showcase the various inspection and debugging capabilities of Adobe Edge Inspect. If you are a seasoned developer and you want to skip this section, you can continue from the *Open the Edge Inspect web inspector window* section and directly start looking at how to debug your mobile web application. But, it is better if you continue with the flow as building the demo app will not take much of your time.

Now, let's get started by creating a directory named `adobe_inspect_test` inside your local web server's webroot directory. Since I have the WAMP server installed on my Windows computer, I have created the directory inside the www folder (which is the webroot for the WAMP server). Create a new empty HTML file named `index.html` inside the `adobe_inspect_test` directory. Fill it with the following HTML markup:

```
<html>
<head>
    <title>Simple demo</title>
    <meta name="viewport" content="width=device-width, initial-
scale=1.0, minimum-scale=1.0, maximum-scale=1.0"/>
</head>
<body>
```

```
<div id="wrapper">
    <div id="div1" class="divStack"><p>First Div</p></div>
    <div id="div2" class="divStack"><p>Second Div</p></div>
    <div class="divStack">
        <input id="btn1" type="button" value="Button1" />
        <input id="btn2" type="button" value="Button2" />
    </div>
</div>
</body>
</html>
```

From the *Installation* section we remember that Adobe Edge Inspect is compatible with Google Chrome only, so throughout our testing we will be running our demo application in Chrome. As I have also said in the *Installation* section, you may note here that Adobe Edge Inspect cannot open pages from the local filesystem (via the `file:///` protocol), so if you are dragging and dropping your `index.html` page into Chrome then Edge Inspect will not be able to open it in the paired mobile devices. You need to run the page from the web server over HTTP. Now let's check our `index.html` file in Chrome. This is how it looks as of now:

As you can make out we have two `div` elements (#div1 and #div2) and two buttons. We will play around with the two `div` elements, and make changes to their HTML markup and CSS styles when we start remote debugging. And then with our two buttons we will see how we can check JavaScript console log messages remotely. You may also notice the use of the `<meta name="viewport" />` tag in the `head` section of the HTML code block. Let's talk about it a little later. First, let's add some styles to our demo application, as it's not looking attractive at all. As you can see in the previous HTML block, I have already added the class and IDs (which will act as our CSS selectors) to the elements so that I can style them using CSS. Now, add the following CSS style in the `head` section of the `index.html` page:

```css
<style type='text/css' >
    html, body, p, div, br, input{
        margin:0;
        padding:0;
    }
    html,body{
        font-family:Helvetica;
```

```
                font-size:14px;
                font-weight:bold;
                color:#222;
                width:100%;
                height:100%;
        }
        #wrapper{
                width:100%;
                height:100%;
                overflow:hidden;
        }
        .divStack{
                padding:10px;
                margin:20px;
                text-align:center;
        }
        #div1{
                background:#ABA73C;
        }
        #div2{
                background:#606873;
        }
        input[type=button]
        {
                padding:5px;
        }
    </style>
```

Save the file and reload Chrome to see the page with some styles now. The following screenshot shows this:

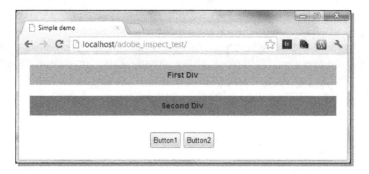

The two `div` elements now have a background color and a boundary. The text is center aligned. The two buttons are also center aligned now.

If you go through the CSS style block, you can see that I have made use of percentage width and height to define the dimensions of our application. This ensures that the elements (especially the two div elements) are adjusted automatically according to the browser window size. So the same application when seen on a mobile device will have the same look and feel with the exact amount of padding and margin, and no elements will be cut off from view. For more responsive designs you can use CSS3 media queries to declare different CSS styles for different devices or screen sizes, but for this very simple demo I preferred to use percentage width and height. For a simple test resize Chrome on your computer and you will see that the elements in the page adjust automatically. The following screenshot shows this:

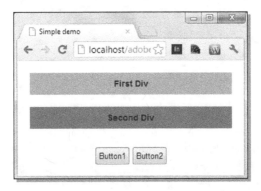

Now, let's focus on the two buttons. I introduced the two buttons into the demo so that we can check out JavaScript console log messages while remote debugging. So, let's add some interactivity to the buttons. Open the index.html file again in your editor and insert this script in the head section of the file:

```
<script type="text/javascript">
        window.addEventListener('load',init,false);

        function init()
        {
            document.getElementById('btn1').addEventListener('click',b
utton1Clicked,false);
            document.getElementById('btn2').addEventListener('click',b
utton2Clicked,false);
        }
        function button1Clicked()
        {
            console.log('Button 1 Clicked');
        }
        function button2Clicked()
        {
            console.log('Button 2 Clicked');
        }
    </script>
```

Save the file and reload. Just for checking things out, let's find out if these two buttons are generating console messages when clicked on. For that, right-click inside Chrome and select **Inspect element**. This will open up the Chrome web developer tools window. Click on the **Console** tab. Now click on the two buttons and you will see console messages based on the button clicked. The following screenshot shows this:

Coming back to the script that we inserted just now inside the index.html file, I have used a DOM level 2 mechanism to register event listeners for the two buttons as well as the browser window object. So whenever the window loads and our DOM is ready, the two buttons get their event handler functions registered. Inside the event listener functions for the buttons (which are button1Clicked() and button2Clicked() respectively) I have defined the corresponding console log messages. So whenever the buttons are clicked a log is generated in the console. With that our demo application is ready to be tested in a mobile device with Adobe Edge Inspect.

Now that you've got with the demo application running in Chrome and your mobile devices paired to your computer (if not then you can look at the *Quick start – pairing mobile devices with your computer* section again), you will instantly see the same page opening in the web view of the Edge Inspect client app in all your mobile devices. The following image shows how the page looks in an iPhone paired to my computer. Note that the page will be displayed inside the Edge Inspect app running on your mobile device.

The viewport meta tag

Before we move on to remote inspection let's talk a little about the `viewport` meta tag that we added earlier in the `head` section of our HTML markup.

Typically, mobile web browsers render a normal web page using a viewport width of 980 px (which is the default for desktop browsers). It then re-scales all the content of the page so that it fits nicely within the mobile browser's visible screen area, which is also called the **viewport**. This makes the web page view very small to read since a mobile device's screen width is less than 980 px and the mobile browser tries to fit the 980 px wide content into its viewport width (for example, 320 px in iPhone browsers). So the user has to zoom in on specific areas of interest and view the content. This normally serves the purpose for most sites. But for mobile optimized sites there may be situations where you want to control the size and scaling of the page. This is where the `viewport` meta tag comes in handy. The `viewport` meta tag allows you to specifically mention a viewport size to which the page will scale. The `viewport` meta tag was introduced by Apple for Mobile Safari to let web developers control the viewport's size and scale. Post Mobile Safari, a lot of other mobile browsers, specifically Webkit-based browsers, also have support for the `viewport` meta tag. The typical syntax is as follows:

```
<meta name="viewport" content="width=device-width, initial-scale=1.0,
minimum-scale=1.0, maximum-scale=1.0"/>
```

`width=device-width` sets the width of the viewport to the device's screen width. The other properties of `initial-scale`, `minimum-scale`, and `maximum-scale` allow the developer to control the scaling of the viewport. A value of `1.0` for `initial-scale` specifies to not do any initial scaling, letting the viewport be of the same size as the device screen. There are a few other properties as well with which you can control how your page would scale. I will not go too deep into the `viewport` meta tag. For now you should continue using it and then explore it further on the Web. Now, let's start debugging.

Open the Edge Inspect web inspector window

Now that you can see our demo application in all your paired mobile devices we are ready to remotely inspect and debug on a targeted mobile device.

Click on the Edge Inspect extension icon in Chrome and select a device for inspection. I am selecting the iPhone from the list of paired devices. Now click on the **Remote Inspection** button to the right of the selected device name. The following image should help you:

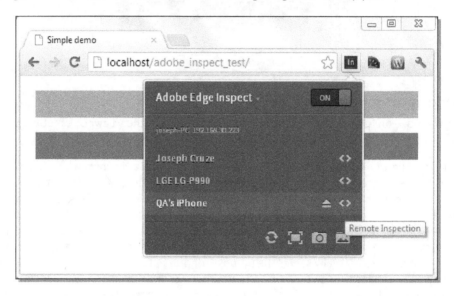

This will open up the Edge Inspect web inspector window also known as the **weinre** (**WEb INspector REmote**) web inspector. This looks very similar to the Chrome web inspector window, doesn't it? So if you have experience with the Chrome web debugging tools then this should look familiar to you:

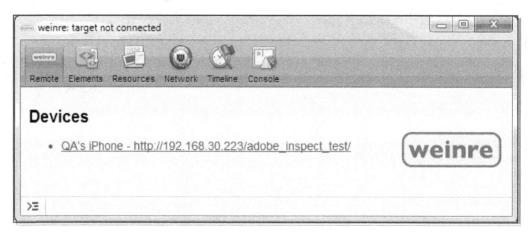

As you can see, by default the **Remote** tab opens up. The title bar says **target not connected**. So, although your mobile device is paired it is not yet ready for remote inspection. Under **Devices** you can see your paired mobile device name with the URL of the page opened in it. Now, click on the device name to connect it. As soon as you do that, you will notice that it turns green. Congratulations! You are now ready for remote inspection as your mobile device is connected. The following screenshot shows this:

You can see the weinre logo on the right. Edge Inspect uses an open source tool called weinre for remote inspection. You can find more information about weinre by following this link: `http://people.apache.org/~pmuellr/weinre/`.

Adobe has hosted an instance of the weinre debug server at `http://debug.edgeinspect.adobe.com/`. This weinre debug server is the most important part of the entire debugging process. What happens is that when you click on the **Remote Inspection** button, the Edge Inspect extension in Chrome reloads the same URL in the paired mobile device and the Edge Inspect app running on your mobile device injects a JavaScript snippet into the page as soon as the target mobile device is connected. This makes the page running in your mobile device act as a debug target and it references the weinre debug API. Both the debug target and the debug client (the Edge Inspect web inspector) communicate with the weinre debug server via **XMLHttpRequest** (**XHR**) and whenever changes are made in the debug client it is instantly reflected in the target mobile device. I wrote a blog post that talks about the weinre server in detail. You can read it here: `http://jbkflex.wordpress.com/2012/04/12/debug-mobile-web-applications-remotely-with-weinre/`.

Changing the HTML markup and viewing the results

Your target mobile device (the iPhone in my case) and the debug client (the Edge Inspect web inspector) are connected to the weinre debug server now and we are ready to make some changes to the HTML. Click on the **Elements** tab in the Edge Inspect web inspector on your computer and you will see the HTML markup of our demo application in it. It may take a few seconds to load since the communication is via Ajax over HTTP. Now, hover your mouse over any element and you will instantly see it being highlighted in your mobile device. For example when I selected the `#div2` (**Second Div**) element in the Edge Inspect web inspector on my computer, it is instantly highlighted on the iPhone.

The following screenshot shows #div2 selected on my computer:

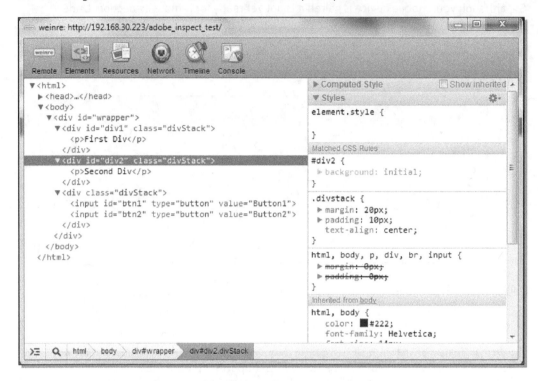

And this corresponding image shows it being highlighted on the iPhone:

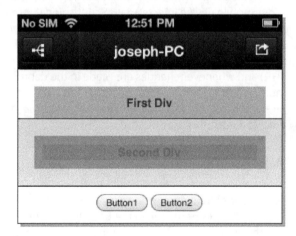

Now let's make some changes to the HTML and see if it is reflected in the target mobile device. Let's change the text inside #div2 from Second Div to Second Div edited. The following screenshot shows the change made in #div2 in the Edge Inspect web inspector on my computer:

And magic! It is changed on the iPhone too. Cool, isn't it? The following screenshot shows the new text inside #div2. This is what remote debugging is all about. We are utilizing the power of Adobe Edge Inspect to overcome the limitations of pure debugging tools in mobile browsers. Instead, you can make changes on your computer and see them directly in your handset.

Let's do another test. Let's remove an element node from the markup. Select the `div` element holding the two buttons. Click on it and press the *Delete* button on your computer keypad. It is temporarily deleted from the DOM tree. The following screenshot shows the DOM state after the node is removed on my computer:

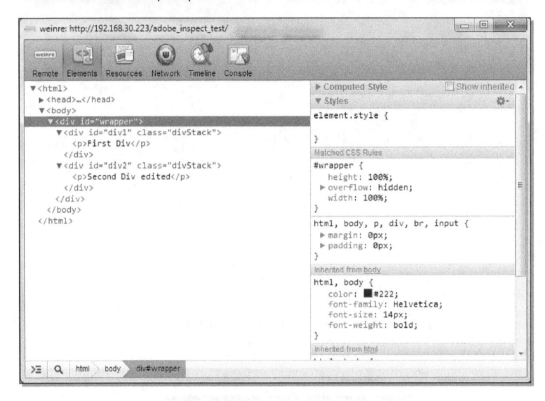

The change can also be seen on the iPhone instantly. The following image shows this:

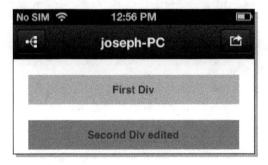

Similarly, you can play around with the HTML markup and check it in the target devices.

Changing CSS style rules

Now, let's make some CSS changes. Select an element in the **Elements** tab and the corresponding CSS styles are listed on the right. Now make changes to the style and the results will reflect on the mobile device as well. I have selected the **First Div** (#div1) element. Let's remove its padding. Uncheck the checkbox against padding and the 10 px padding is removed. The following screenshot shows the CSS change made in the Edge Inspect web inspector on my computer:

And the following image shows the result being reflected on the iPhone instantly:

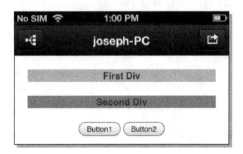

Similarly, you can change other style rules such as width, height, padding, and margin and see the changes directly on your device.

Viewing console log messages

Click on the **Console** tab in the Edge Inspect web inspector to open it. Now click/tap on the buttons one by one on your mobile device. You will see that log messages are being printed on the console for the corresponding button clicked/tapped on the mobile device. This way you can debug JavaScript code remotely. Although Edge Inspect lacks JavaScript debugging using breakpoints (which would have been really handy had we been able to watch local and global variables, and function arguments by pausing the execution and observing the state) but nevertheless, by using the console messages you can at least know that your JavaScript code is executing correctly to the point where the log is generated. So basic script debugging can be done. The following screenshot shows the console messages printed remotely from the paired iPhone:

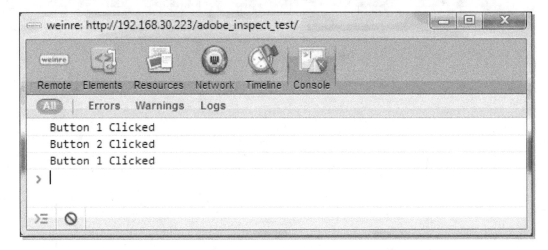

Similarly you can target another device for remote inspection and see the changes directly in the device. And with that we have covered how to remotely debug web applications running on a mobile device.

Remote inspection for multiple devices

You have seen how I targeted one mobile device (the iPhone) for remote inspection and then using the Edge Inspect web inspector I remotely debugged the demo application. Now, you might be thinking that we paired multiple devices but during remote inspection we selected only one. One thing to note here is that you have to target mobile devices individually for remote inspection. It's not that there is a common Edge Inspect web inspector for all the paired mobile devices such that you debug in it and the changes are reflected simultaneously in all devices. Instead for every paired mobile device you have to open the Edge Inspect web inspector separately and only one instance of the web inspector will run.

For example, this time I have selected the Android device for remote inspection from the list of paired devices. Using the same methods that I discussed previously you can also target and connect another device for remote inspection.

The following image shows `Button1` being selected in the Edge Inspect web inspector on my computer:

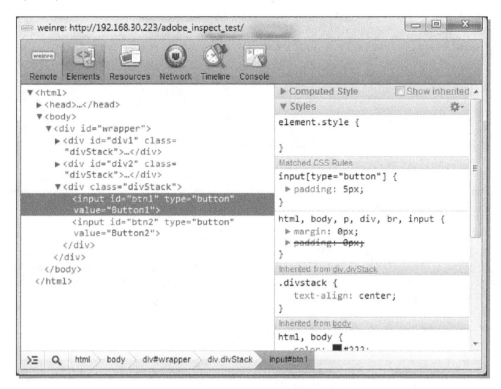

And the corresponding image shows the selected button being highlighted in the Android device:

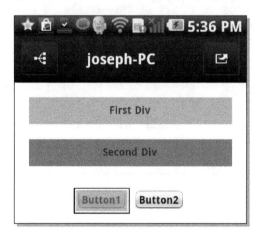

Debugging already hosted mobile web projects

You have your mobile web project already hosted on a live server. You have deployed your project before Adobe Edge Inspect came out and did not really use remote inspection techniques to test your application. So what can you do now? There is not a problem at all. Just browse to your project URL in Chrome on your computer and it will open in all the paired Edge Inspect mobile devices. Now, target any paired device for remote inspection and follow the steps mentioned in the previous section for debugging.

Use your own weinre server

With Adobe Edge Inspect you can use your own weinre debug server for remote inspection. This will improve performance, speed up connection time, and will keep the remote inspection traffic local. So if you have a local instance of the weinre server running on your computer or on your local network, you can use that as a debug server instead of using the default weinre server hosted by Adobe.

To use your own weinre server, first of all you will need to have the weinre server set up on your computer. For that you will need the weinre JAR file and Java installed on your computer. This is out of the scope of this book but I have written a detailed post on setting up and running a local weinre server here: `http://jbkflex.wordpress.com/2012/04/12/debug-mobile-web-applications-remotely-with-weinre/`. You can read it if you like.

After you have a weinre server set up locally, you can follow these steps to use it with Edge Inspect:

1. Right-click on the Edge Inspect extension icon in Chrome and select **Options**. The following screenshot shows this:

    This will open up the **Options** page in Chrome.

2. Now in the **Weinre Server** section select the **Custom** option from the drop-down list.

3. Enter the path of your weinre server in the textbox that appears and then save it.

The following screenshot shows the **Options** page with a custom weinre server path:

From now on, Edge Inspect will use your local weinre debug server. You can again revert back to the default weinre server by selecting Default (Adobe) on the select list.

Cache management

You can individually clear the cache and refresh the page in the paired mobile devices by tapping on the **Refresh** button in the Edge Inspect mobile app menu on your mobile device. The following screenshot shows the **Refresh** feature on an iPhone:

You can also refresh and clear the cache for all the paired mobile devices by clicking on the **Refresh all devices** button (the first button at the bottom) in the Edge Inspect browser extension in Chrome. The following screenshot shows this:

Taking screenshots

Take a screenshot of the page on one paired mobile device by tapping on the **Screenshot** button (fourth from the top) in the Edge Inspect mobile app menu as shown in the following image:

You can also take screenshots of the page in all the connected mobile devices by clicking on the **Request screenshots** button (the third button at the bottom) in the Edge Inspect extension in Chrome. The following image should help you out:

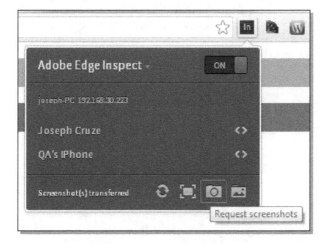

By default, screenshots are saved in the Edge Inspect subfolder in the Documents (Mac OS X) or My Documents (Windows) directory , which you can view by clicking on the **Open folder containing screenshots** button (the fourth button at the bottom) in the Edge Inspect extension in Chrome. The following image shows it. All the screenshots are saved in the folder with some metadata in separate text files.

You can also specify your own folder to save the screenshots. For that follow these steps:

1. Right-click on the Edge Inspect extension icon in Chrome and select **Options**.
2. Then under the **Screenshots Folder** section click on the **Edit** button.
3. Enter the path of the folder where you want to save the screenshots and then save it.

The following image shows the process:

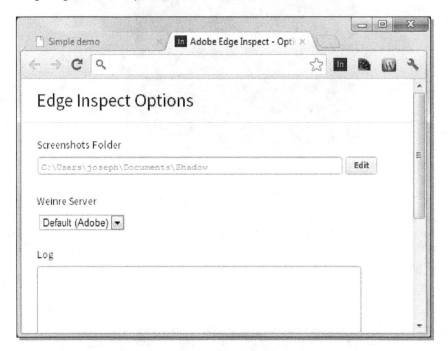

Toggle full screen view on mobile devices

With a single click on the full screen toggle button (the second button at the bottom) in the Chrome Extension menu on your computer you can toggle between the full screen views on all your paired mobile devices. The following screenshot shows the full screen toggle button in Chrome:

So when you click for full screen view, the menu bar in the Edge Inspect mobile app is hidden. This provides more real estate or viewport height to test your projects. The following image shows the resultant view in the paired iPhone after the full screen button is clicked in the Chrome extension:

Debugging pages with authentication and login

When you browse a page in Chrome that requires HTTP authentication, you will see a login form in the paired Edge Inspect devices. Enter the same username and password to open the page in the connected mobile device. After that you can start remote inspection and debugging as usual. The following screenshot shows this:

SSL support

Use unsigned SSL certificates during development. When your browse a page in Chrome that requires you to accept a certificate, the connected Edge Inspect devices will provide a dialog prompting you to accept an unsigned certificate. After accepting the certificate on your mobile you can start remote inspection. The following screenshot shows this:

People and places you should get to know

If you need help with Adobe Edge Inspect, here are some people and places that will prove invaluable:

Official sites

You can visit the following official sites if you want to learn more about Edge Inspect, to know more about new features and keep yourself updated with the latest releases:

+ Homepage: http://html.adobe.com/edge/inspect/
+ Features: http://html.adobe.com/edge/inspect/features.html
+ Manual and documentation: http://forums.adobe.com/docs/DOC-2535
+ Tech specs: http://html.adobe.com/edge/inspect/tech-specs.html
+ Downloads: http://creative.adobe.com/join/starter
+ Blog: http://blogs.adobe.com/edgeinspect/

Articles and tutorials

Here is a list of five good articles and tutorials that you can refer to:

+ A video overview from *Create the Web Keynote* by Adobe: http://www.youtube.com/watch?v=SyzZHS-1fPE&feature=player_embedded
+ A blog post of mine: http://jbkflex.wordpress.com/2012/09/27/adobe-shadow-is-now-adobe-edge-inspect/
+ Another blog post of mine: http://jbkflex.wordpress.com/2012/08/28/use-your-own-weinre-server-with-adobe-shadow-step-by-step/
+ A tutorial by Holly Schinsky (Developer Evangelist at Adobe): http://devgirl.org/2012/06/04/adobe-shadow-inspectdebug-your-mobile-web-content/
+ A tutorial by Brian Rinaldi (Content and Community Manager in Developer Relations at Adobe Systems, and a programmer): http://www.adobe.com/devnet/edge-inspect/articles/browser-testing-across-devices-with-adobe-edge-inspect.html

Community

Find out what others are doing with Adobe Edge Inspect and speak to experts directly by subscribing to the following communities:

- Official forums: `http://forums.adobe.com/community/edge_inspect`
- User FAQ: `http://html.adobe.com/edge/inspect/faq.html`
- Facebook page: `http://www.facebook.com/EdgeInspect`
- Follow on Twitter: `https://twitter.com/EdgeInspect`

Blogs

A list of up to five influential and important people in the world of the technology whose blogs would be useful to subscribe to are as follows:

- The blog of Christian Cantrell, Product Manager and Application Developer of the Web Platform team, Adobe: `http://blogs.adobe.com/cantrell/`
- The blog of Adobe Web Platform team: `http://blogs.adobe.com/webplatform/`
- Find out about all of the different HTML projects that Adobe is working on and how Adobe is contributing to open web standards; you can also contribute: `http://html.adobe.com/`
- The blog of Raymond Camden (Developer Evangelist at Adobe): `http://www.raymondcamden.com/`
- The blog of Brian Rinaldi (Content and Community Manager in Developer Relations at Adobe Systems, and a programmer): `http://remotesynthesis.com/`
- The blog of Amit Kishnani (Senior Software Engineer, Adobe Shadow team): `http://blogs.adobe.com/edgeinspect/author/akishnan/`

Twitter

A list of up to five influential and important people in the world of technology whose tweets would be useful to follow are as follows:

- Follow Bruce Bowman (Senior Product Manager, Adobe Edge Inspect): `http://twitter.com/brucebowman`
- Follow Duane O'Brien (developer and Agile coach for Adobe, works on Adobe Edge Inspect) on Twitter: `https://twitter.com/DuaneOBrien`

✦ Follow Patrick Mueller (Creator of the weinre tool, IBMer working on emerging technologies on Web StuffTM) on Twitter: `https://twitter.com/pmuellr`

✦ Follow Christian Cantrell (Product Manager and Application Developer of the Web Platform Team, Adobe) on Twitter: `http://twitter.com/cantrell`

✦ Follow Holly Schinsky (Developer Evangelist at Adobe, passionate about mobile development) on Twitter: `http://twitter.com/devgirlFL`

✦ For more open source information, follow Packt at `http://twitter.com/#!/packtopensource`

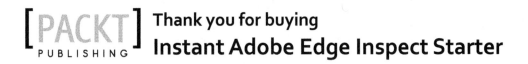

Thank you for buying
Instant Adobe Edge Inspect Starter

About Packt Publishing

Packt, pronounced 'packed', published its first book "*Mastering phpMyAdmin for Effective MySQL Management*" in April 2004 and subsequently continued to specialize in publishing highly focused books on specific technologies and solutions.

Our books and publications share the experiences of your fellow IT professionals in adapting and customizing today's systems, applications, and frameworks. Our solution based books give you the knowledge and power to customize the software and technologies you're using to get the job done. Packt books are more specific and less general than the IT books you have seen in the past. Our unique business model allows us to bring you more focused information, giving you more of what you need to know, and less of what you don't.

Packt is a modern, yet unique publishing company, which focuses on producing quality, cutting-edge books for communities of developers, administrators, and newbies alike. For more information, please visit our website: www.packtpub.com.

Writing for Packt

We welcome all inquiries from people who are interested in authoring. Book proposals should be sent to author@packtpub.com. If your book idea is still at an early stage and you would like to discuss it first before writing a formal book proposal, contact us; one of our commissioning editors will get in touch with you.

We're not just looking for published authors; if you have strong technical skills but no writing experience, our experienced editors can help you develop a writing career, or simply get some additional reward for your expertise.

Selenium Testing Tools Cookbook

ISBN: 978-1-84951-574-0   Paperback: 326 pages

Over 90 recipes to build, maintain, and improve test automation with Selenium WebDriver

1. Learn to leverage the power of Selenium WebDriver with simple examples that illustrate real world problems and their workarounds

2. Each sample demonstrates key concepts allowing you to advance your knowledge of Selenium WebDriver in a practical and incremental way

3. Explains testing of mobile web applications with Selenium Drivers for platforms such as iOS and Android

Learning Modernizr

ISBN: 978-1-78216-022-9   Paperback: 118 pages

Create forward-compatible websites using feature detection features of Modernizr

1. Build a progressive experience using a vast array of detected CSS3 features

2. Replace images with CSS based counterparts

3. Learn the benefits of detecting features instead of checking the name and version of the browser and serving accordingly

Please check **www.PacktPub.com** for information on our titles